LEGENDARY CREATURES of MYTH and MAGIC

by **MARIANNA MAYER**
Illustrated by **MICHAEL HAGUE**

MADISON
PARK PRESS™

NEW YORK

For Bethany Cobb
　　　　　—M.M.

For Scott Hague
　　　　　—M.H.

elcome to the amazing world of myth and magic. Here you will meet a variety of the most amazing legendary creatures—from ancient deities once worshipped as gods and goddesses, to animal culture heroes, monsters, and supernatural beings who were once either feared or accepted as real. In fact, some may have actually existed once upon a time, and still others may even exist today. Yet all of them have haunted and inspired humankind's dreams and fantasies for more than 30,000 years.

The list of creatures covered in this book is certainly not complete—a list that included every being drawn from myth, legend, and folklore from every age and culture would extend to thousands of entries. I selected some of my favorites, and hope this book will encourage you to continue to explore the whole world of fabulous creatures for yourself.

Meanwhile I'll leave it to you to decide which of these astonishing creatures still walk among us today, and which are the stuff of legend and dreams.

—Marianna Mayer

Chimaera and Pegasus

The Chimaera keeps well hidden inside his black cave on the side of a sheer cliff that plunges down to the sea. If hungry, the monster needs only to descend to ravage and burn the countryside, devouring people and animals at will. An indomitable opponent, he has the tail and claws of a dragon, iron-tough scales covering a giant goat's body, and the head of a fire-breathing lion.

The Greek hero Bellerophon enlisted winged Pegasus to fly him to the Chimaera's lair. To put an end to the pillage, the hero riding Pegasus drove his spear into the single vulnerable spot beneath the Chimaera's armored body . . . his heart.

Against flames, and razor-sharp claws, winged horse and rider battled. Until, at daybreak, with his strength waning, Bellerophon struck the deathblow. The spear met its mark and pierced the monster to its very heart. The roaring ceased, the flames faded to billowing smoke, and finally blew away. The Chimaera's lifeless body fell down, down, down to the waiting sea below, swallowed by the waves to disappear forever.

Lamb Plant

The Lamb Plant develops from a kind of round melon seed. The lamb is encapsulated within the fruit of the plant. When ripe, the fruit bursts open, revealing the little lamb. The plant matures to a height of three feet with a head, ears, eyes, and all other parts of a newly born lamb. It remains rooted by its navel in the middle of its belly, and while it grows it feeds on the surrounding plants. The lamb's wool is so white and soft that it is most prized.

Descriptions of the Lamb Plant differ little, and for centuries it was considered fact. In the late eighteenth century botanists still maintained the existence of the Lamb Plant or *vegetable lamb*.

Abatwa

The Abatwa are so tiny that they are difficult to see. If you want to find one, look between blades of grass. The Abatwa ride ants without saddles or reins. They prefer to roam, setting up temporary camps inside anthills. Their favorite food is cow meat, which they are highly unlikely to find.

When meeting an Abatwa, know they are sensitive about their size. For example, an Abatwa might ask, "Where did you first see me?" It is best to pretend that he is tall. So answer, "From a distance or some high hilltop." If you answer that you spotted him right here at your foot, he will try to kill you with a poison dart. In the Abatwa's Zulu homeland, stepping on one is certain to bring about your death.

Cerberus

Legend tells us that within the very depths of the Underworld, at the very gates of Acheron, the three-headed dog Cerberus stands guard for his grim master, Hades, Lord of the Dead. When the dead descend to Tartarus, if they have the fare, they are ferried across the waters of the River Styx. And, there at the gates of the opposite shore stands the watchful guard Cerberus. Only the famed musician and poet Orpheus, in search of his lost love, was known to charm the fierce beast.

Baba Yaga

Baba Yaga of Russian folklore still lives in a small clearing deep in the birch forest. No one knows how old she is; she has always lived in that forest.

Baba Yaga is very tall and thin, and she is always hungry. Humans are her preferred food. Leftover human bones were used to make her crooked hut, which stands high above ground on giant chicken legs that can spin it around at the whim of its mistress. Be assured, Baba Yaga lives alone.

Baba Yaga's favorite means of transport is a giant mortar and pestle. Streaking through the air at lightning speed, she stands in the mortar while using the pestle as navigator.

Leshy

The Leshy hails from Russia, as well as many other eastern European lands. By all accounts the Leshy is a most endearing green and purple creature. Gigantic while within the forest, it transforms to the tiniest being when beyond the sheltering trees. Many a wanderer lost in the deep wood has been guided back upon his path to home by the helpful Leshy.

Fafner, the Dragon

Fafner, the wingless dragon of Norse myth, and son of the King of Dwarfs, had once been a dwarf himself. Fafner coveted the magnificent treasure the gods had entrusted to his father. To obtain it, the son killed his father, and for such a shameful crime, Fafner was transformed into a dragon.

Fafner slithered away with his stolen bloodstained treasure to the deepest cave, content to live in isolated darkness. Draped over his gold and jewels, Fafner lay slumbering for many long years, confident there was no one alive who could defeat him.

Then the hero Sigurd came to do battle. What Sigurd lacked in size he had in intelligence. Sigurd dug a ditch outside the cave. The task completed, Sigurd with sword at the ready hid in that ditch. *"Fafner, you vile worm,"* he called. *"Come out and fight."*

Fafner sprang roaring from the cave. Sigurd was nowhere to be seen. The dragon strode over to the ditch and stopped, searching for his challenger. He was standing over Sigurd, though he did not know it. Sigurd seized his chance and, thrusting his sword into the dragon's soft underbelly, he pierced Fafner to the very heart. It was a mortal blow; Fafner fell dead, and his beloved ill-gotten treasure passed on to Sigurd.

Baku

The Baku are spirits having the head of an elephant and the body of a lion, but like most spirits, they are fond of shape-shifting, making it difficult to settle on any one description. Spirits are after all a changeable race by nature.

The main thing to know about the Baku is that they will very gladly help humans by eating nightmares or the evil spirits who create nasty dreams. Often they do this without our knowing; other times a nightmare sufferer can awaken and call upon a Baku to eat the nightmare. Even today, Baku depictions are placed in Japanese bedrooms to guard against terrible dreams. And the Chinese often write the characters for Baku upon their pillow to ensure peaceful slumber.

Centaur

The Centaur is a magnificent creature—part man, part horse. Female or male, she or he has a horse's body with all four legs, but its head, torso, and arms are that of a human. The human frame is thus joined at the waist to the horse's muscular shoulders.

The Centaur can possess a fiercely wild, unfriendly nature or a wise and kindly one. They are a most helpful ally in time of war, combining great speed, strength, and dexterity, as demonstrated in C. S. Lewis's *The Chronicles of Narnia.*

It is theorized that the idea of a race of Centaurs came from the reaction of a non-horse-riding culture to their first sighting of men on horseback.

Unicorn

In a distant fabled land, on any given morning the Unicorn goes down to the golden fountain to drink, the very spot where all the good animals come to drink. The Unicorn is as white as freshly fallen snow. He looks much like an elegant white horse. Were it not for his long spiral horn you might easily mistake him for one, but he most certainly is not.

It is said that if the Unicorn chooses to dip his horn into poison he could neutralize it. The Unicorn is a fabulous wild creature, good yet fierce, selfless yet solitary; legend tells that only a gentle and true maiden can tame him. As soon as the Unicorn sees her, he lays his head in her lap and falls asleep. The Unicorn is also well loved for his ability to mend broken hearts, and turn tears of sorrow to tears of joy.

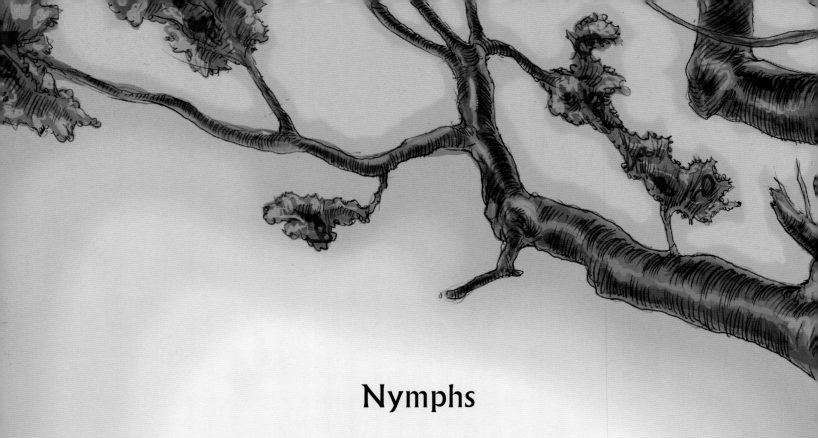

Nymphs

Once upon a time every part of the countryside was inhabited by magical beings, most notably Nymphs of all varieties.

There are Nymphs known as Dryads, who live in and protect trees. More specifically, the Hamadryads are at home in oak trees, and the Meliades in fruit trees. Tree Nymphs actually are part of their beloved tree, and seldom if ever leave it.

The Naiades dwell in streams, rivers, and ponds. The Limoniades are the guardians of meadows, while the Limniades protect marshes and the Oreades look after mountains. At the same time, Nereides make their home down in the depths of the sea, and Hyades live high up in the clouds.

In ancient Greek legend, the hero Perseus asked the Naiades for *the cloak of darkness*, which made its wearer invisible—this precious treasure had been entrusted to the Naiades for safekeeping by the gods. Once Perseus explained that he needed it to defeat Medusa, the Naiades granted his request on the condition that he return the cloak once the perilous challenge was completed.

Medusa and Her Sisters

Medusa was one of three Gorgon Sisters; the ancient Greeks believed she was the only mortal among them. Her deathless sisters were Harpies—bird-like creatures with serpent scales, hands of brass, and powerful wings. Born an exquisite beauty, Medusa only grew more beautiful as she matured. Indeed she had no want of suitors—mortal or immortal.

Medusa chose to look after the temple of Venus, a jealous goddess by all accounts. As Venus's servant, she had to swear never to wed. Yet Poseidon, who was the great god of the sea, desired and pursued her. Though Medusa was innocent of any wrongdoing, Poseidon's interest enraged Venus. And, to punish Medusa, Venus transformed the maiden into a monster more terrible than her two horrifying Harpy Sisters. Now Medusa's flame-red hair writhed with poisonous vipers, and one glimpse of her bewitching face turned anyone to stone.

Phoenix

According to the ancient Greek historian Herodotus, the Phoenix best resembles the eagle in shape and size. Though not a giant bird, the Phoenix is most certainly extraordinary. It appears in Egypt only once every five hundred years. Thought to be an immortal bird, when the Phoenix feels all strength waning, it finally builds a nest and lays a single luminous egg. When the egg is about to hatch, the nest and aged Phoenix burst into magnificent flame. As the last lick of fire subsides, a newborn Phoenix emerges out of the smoldering ash.

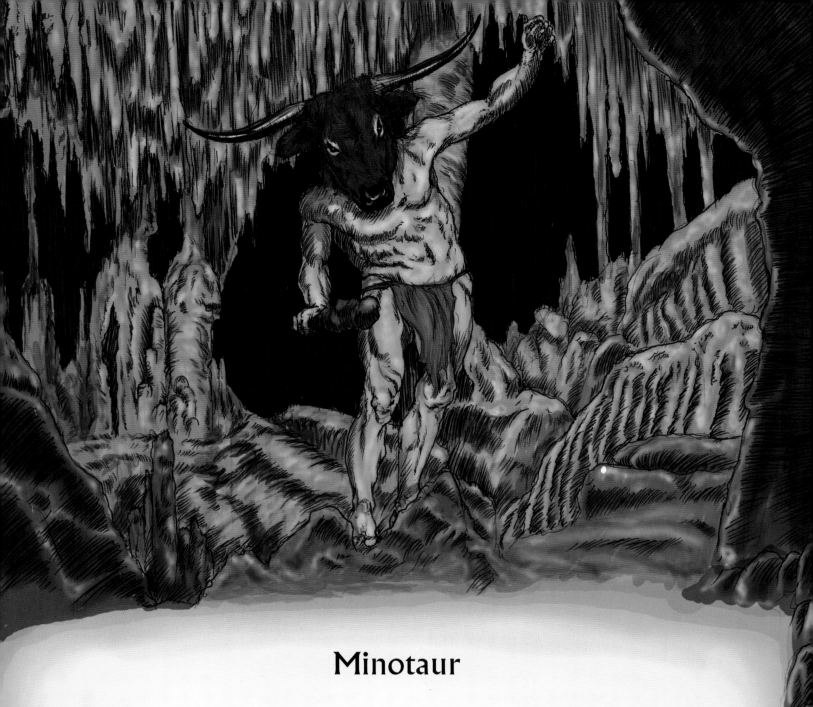

Minotaur

The ancient Greek legends tell of a slow-moving hulk of a monster, the Minotaur, with his muscular man's body and head of a great horned bull. Upon the isle of Crete a sprawling underground maze was created to imprison him, and there he was left to lurk.

Every nine years, a human sacrifice was offered to appease the Minotaur. Victims were forced down into the maze, and what became of them no one knew. Except for Theseus, the son of Poseidon.

Cast down into the labyrinth with only a skein of thread to aid him, Theseus unrolled the thread as he wandered. When the Minotaur struck, the youth's quickness and ability defeated the sluggish beast. Triumphant, Theseus needed only to follow the thread he had laid out to regain his freedom.

Fenris

Fenris, the Wolf of Fenrir, is a creature of giant proportions—the third offspring of Loki, the mischievous Norse god, and his wife, the ogress Angerboda. Fearing him, the Norse gods confined Fenris to an isolated island in the middle of a lake surrounded by a forest of iron trees.

There they hoped Fenris would do the least harm. Yet the wolf only grew larger and larger. Realizing he would soon break free, the gods tried to chain him. Fenris was too strong; even the combined strength of the gods could not constrain him. So the gods enlisted the help of the gnomes, for they too were afraid of the terrible beast. The gnomes made a spell to bind Fenris. It combined the sound of a cat's paw, the sigh of a fish, the saliva of a bird, a single hair from a woman's beard, and the root of a mountain—these were then spun together and bound with the muscle of a bear.

But legend tells that the chains and spell are only temporary. Fenris's hunger grows greater with time, so that one day it is said he will break free and devour the world and everything in it.

Pooka

Don't be surprised if, while walking through the woods in the wee hours, a Pooka should suddenly rise up beneath you and carry you off for a wild ride, only to finally dump you into a muddy pond without so much as a howdy-do. If you maintain your sense of humor even after such undignified treatment, the Pooka may in turn reward you.

Exclusive to Ireland, the Pooka is found at twilight in secluded woodland haunts. The Pooka enjoys appearing suddenly and is a great prankster. It can adopt many forms, but most often assumes the shape of a dark-colored animal—horse, mule, bull, donkey, goat, or giant dog with smoldering amber eyes.

Roc

Tales of a gigantic bird called the Roc can be found among the stories included in *The Arabian Nights*. During one of Sindbad's voyages, the famed sailor encountered these extraordinary birds as he explored the Isle of the Rocs. When Sindbad first came upon a Roc egg, it was so huge he thought it was a magnificent doomed building. In fact, in flight the adult Roc can blot out the very sun, casting a shadow that makes day seem like the darkest night. Sindbad declared that he saw one of these powerful birds fly off carrying an elephant. A single feather from a Roc's wing is seventy feet long.

Cyclops

A race of giants resembling humans, the Cyclops had but a single eye centered just above the bridge of his nose. Savage man-eater, the Cyclops makes his home in caves upon an island along unchartered waters.

The Seven Voyages of Sindbad the Sailor describes a terrifying encounter with a Cyclops. During this adventure, Sindbad and his shipmates are shipwrecked upon the island of the Cyclops, and taken prisoner. Before everyone is devoured—bones and all—Sindbad outsmarts the dull-witted creature by managing to blind it with a well-aimed spear. Afterward he and the remaining survivors make a desperate break for freedom and successfully sail away on a raft.

A horrific Cyclops was also known to threaten the ancient Greek hero Odysseus and his loyal crew in *The Odyssey,* a classic Greek myth of epic proportions.

Faun

An untamed spirit, the Faun lives in remote woodlands. At one time, the Faun and the Satyr were described as different creatures. Both have horns and goat-like bodies below the waist and human above, but the Faun is said to have a goat's hooves and the Satyr has feet. Today they are thought to be similar, if not exactly the same.

Ancient Romans believed in Faunus, a goat-like god, and the Ancient Greeks worshipped Pan, the protector of shepherds and their flock.

Natural and carefree, a Faun plays hypnotic tunes upon his panpipes. If you hear their music while in the woods, you will likely fall into a deep sleep and have some splendid dreams to recall upon waking.

Puck

Puck is said to be the very last of England's faerie folk. Also known as Robin Goodfellow, Puck assists Oberon, the King of Faeries. A trickster by nature, Puck does his work by moonlight.

When not making mischief, Puck can be induced to do good works. For example, he might aid some needy old woman—churn the butter, card the wool, thresh the wheat, or clean the house—all whilst she sleeps. If you are clever you might gain his favor. He has a fondness for fresh cream and would willingly accept your kind offer of a cup.

Puck can take the shape of animals, but like his counterpart Pan, he often has the hindquarters and cloven hooves of a goat.

Kelpie

Beware. In Scotland they say the legendary Kelpie should be avoided at all costs. A wild mythic horse, the Kelpie is found in the dead of night on the windy moors of Scotland. Should an unwitting stranger approach, the Kelpie at first seems friendly enough, even tame. But if a person is so foolish as to risk a ride upon the Kelpie's back, the once gentle horse transforms into a wild fire-breathing beast with smoldering red coals for eyes. Up and away in a flash, the Kelpie's victim is driven into the sea to meet his doom.

Book design by Christos Peterson

Published by Madison Park Press, 15 East 26th Street,
New York, New York 10010.

ISBN: 978-1-58288-245-1

Printed in China